I0012012

80 SOLVED CASES OF

STADISTICS IN

DAX LANGUAGE

POWER BI

Business Intelligence

Ramón J. Castro

© Rebel Out Post Publications
©80 Solved Cases of Statistics in DAX Language

First edition (2023)

©Autor: Ramón Javier Castro Amador (2023)
©Cover designed by: Ramón Javier Castro Amador (2023)

Copyright: 2306094544160-7NKW3S
Web: www.facebook.com/80solvedcasesofstadisticindax
Email: publicaciones.rebel.out.post@gmail.com

No part of this publication, including the design, may be reproduced, stored or transmitted in any form or by any means, electronic, mechanical, optical, recording or photocopying, without the prior express permission of the author.

The lack of success in the past
doesn't guarantee failure in the future.

Index

Introduction

"80 Solved Statistical Cases in DAX Language" is the third release in a series of four quick guides designed to address multiple scenarios using the DAX language. At the moment, our collection includes:

- 180 Solved Cases in Dax Language
- 90 Solved Cases on Time Intelligence in Dax
- 60 Solved Cases on Finance in Dax (in press)

Following the practical approach of the previous guides, this new edition is aimed at Microsoft Power BI users and presents a total of 87 statistical case studies solved with DAX. The selected examples seek to address the most common situations in the business environment.

All DAX code provided in this guide can be tested using the file **"80_solved_cases_of_statistic_in_dax.pbix"**, available for download at the following link:

https://acortar.link/tyPT8b

Finally, it should be noted that the statistical analysis presented in this book is based on time periods. Therefore, it is essential to have a Calendar Table in the model. The code needed to create such a table is found in Case 1 of this work.

Solved cases

001. Create CALENDAR table
Table tools > new table

STEP 1

```
Calendary =
ADDCOLUMNS (
        //start date, end date
        CALENDAR ( MIN ( Sales[Date] ), TODAY () ),
        //numerical values
        "year", YEAR ( [Date] ),
        "month", MONTH ( [Date] ),
        "day", DAY ( [Date] ),
        "quarter", QUARTER ( [Date] ),
        "weekDay", WEEKDAY ( [Date] ),
        "weekNum", WEEKNUM ( [Date] ),
        //values in text
        "monthName", FORMAT ( [Date], "MMM" ),
        "weekDayName", FORMAT ( [Date], "DDD" ),
        "quarterName", SWITCH ( QUARTER ( [Date] ), 1,
        "First", 2, "Second", 3, "Third", 4, "quarter")
)
```

STEP 2

Once the table is finished, it must be marked as a calendar table. To do this we will do the following:

1. Right-click on the table icon.
2. Select the option "Mark as date table".

2

002. Population

STEP 1

Population is defined as a set of similar elements or events that are of interest for some question or experiment.

For this case the population is going to be made up of all apartments located in the city of BEDOK with three or more bedrooms since 1990.

Table tools > new table

Apartments in BEDOK's town with 3 or more rooms from 1990 =
CALCULATETABLE(
    //table or expression returning a table
    'DATASET-Singapore Flat Prices',
    //conditions
    'DATASET-Singapore Flat Prices'[town] = "BEDOK",
    'DATASET-Singapore Flat Prices'[roomNumber] >= 3,
    'DATASET-Singapore Flat Prices'[Year of construction]
    >= "1990"
)

STEP 2

Calculation of the total population.

Modeling > new measure

Population =
COUNTROWS(
'Apartments in BEDOK''s town with 3 or more rooms from 1990'
)

003. Sample size (finite populations)
Modeling > new measure

```
Sampling Size =
//population size
VAR N = COUNTROWS('Apartments in BEDOK''s town with
3 or more rooms since 1990')

//for a 95% confidence level
VAR confidence_Level = 0.95

//alpha value
VAR alfaValue = (1- confidence_Level)/2

//accumulated probability
VAR Fz = confidence_Level + alfaValue

//Z_alfa
VAR Z_alfa = NORM.S.INV( Fz )

//for an accuracy of 3%
VAR d =  0.03

//expected 5% share
VAR p = 0.05

//calculation of the value of q
VAR q = 1 - p

return

DIVIDE(
    N * POWER(Z_alfa,2) * p * q ,
    POWER(d,2) * (N-1) + POWER(Z_alfa,2) * p * q
)
```

004. Random data sample

This case continues from the result obtained in case 2.

STEP 1

A sample is made up of a given number of subjects or things extracted from a population.

Table tools > new table

```
Purchase sample prices =
//a variable is generated to define the sample size and
characterization
VAR data =
SAMPLE(
    //sample size
    100,
    //table or expression returning a table
    'Apartments in BEDOK''s town with 3 or more rooms
    since 1990',
    //column from which the sample is obtained
    'Apartments in BEDOK''s town with 3 or more rooms
    since 1990'[Purchase price],
    //order
    ASC
)

return

//creates a table from the variable containing the final
result
SELECTCOLUMNS(
    //table
    data,
    //columns
    "Year", [Year of construction],
    "Town", [town],
    "roomNumber", [roomNumber],
```

```
    "Prices", [Purchase price]
)
```

This case continues from the result obtained in case 2.

Table tools > new table

```
Ten sample prices by rooms Number =
//data range delimit
VAR orderTable =
ALL( 'Apartments in BEDOK''s town with 3 or more rooms
      since 1990'
)

//select the category column
VAR Categories =
SELECTCOLUMNS(
    //table
    ALL('Apartments in BEDOK''s town with 3 or more
    rooms since 1990'[roomNumber]),
    //columns
    "roomNumberCat", [roomNumber]
)

//generate random series
VAR sampleData =
GENERATE(
    Categories,
    VAR curCat = [roomNumberCat]
    VAR tempTable =
    FILTER(
        //table or expression returning a table
        orderTable,
        //filter
```

```
        [roomNumber] = curCat)

return

//result table
SAMPLE(
        //number of values
        10,
        //table or expression returning a table
        tempTable,
        TRUE(),
        //order
        ASC
)
```

006. Sampling error
Modeling > new measure

```
Sampling error =
//confidence level
VAR confidence_Level = 0.95

//alpha value
VAR alfaValue = (1- confidence_Level)/2

//accumulated probability
VAR Fz = confidence_Level + alfaValue

//inverse normal distribution
VAR inverseNormalDistribution = NORM.S.INV( Fz )

//population table
Apartments in BEDOK's town with 3 or more rooms from
1990 =
CALCULATETABLE(
        //table or expression returning a table
```

```
    'DATASET-Singapore Flat Prices',
    //conditions
    'DATASET-Singapore Flat Prices'[town] = "BEDOK",
    'DATASET-Singapore Flat Prices'[roomNumber] >= 3,
    'DATASET-Singapore Flat Prices'[Year of construction]
    >= "1990"
)

//population standard deviation
VAR sampleStandarDesv =
STDEV.S( 'Apartments in BEDOK''s town with 3 or more
         rooms since 1990'[Purchase price]
 )

//sample size
VAR sampleSize =
COUNTROWS('Apartments in BEDOK''s town with 3 or
              more rooms since 1990'
)

return

inverseNormalDistribution *
DIVIDE( sampleStandarDesv,  SQRT(sampleSize) )
```

007. Confidence interval -Normal
Modeling > new measure

```
Confidence interval (Normal) -weight (kg) Singapore's
population =
//sample size
VAR samplingSize =
COUNTROWS( 'DATASET-Singapore Population' )

//standard deviation
VAR stdDesv =
```

```
STDEV.S( 'DATASET-Singapore Population'[Weight (kg)] )

//95% confidence level
VAR ConfInterval =
DIVIDE(
        //numerator
        100-95,
        //denominator
        100
)

return

CONFIDENCE.NORM(
    //confidence level
    ConfInterval,
    //standard deviation
    stdDesv,
    //sample size
    samplingSize
)
```

008. Confidence interval -T

Modeling > new measure

```
Confidence interval (T) -weight (kg) Singapore's
population =
//sample size
VAR samplingSize =
COUNTROWS( 'DATASET-Singapore Population' )

//standard deviation
VAR stdDesv =
STDEV.S( 'DATASET-Singapore Population'[Weight (kg)] )

//95% confidence level
```

```
VAR ConfInterval =
DIVIDE(
        //numerator
        100-95,
        //denominator
        100
)

return

CONFIDENCE.T(
    //confidence level
    ConfInterval,
    //standard deviation
    stdDesv,
    //sample size
    samplingSize
)
```

009. Average
Modeling > new measure

```
Average M² per flat =
//expression
AVERAGE(
        'DATASET-Singapore Flat Prices'[floor_area_M2]
)
```

010. Accumulated average
Modeling > new measure

```
Cumulative average purchase price per year =
CALCULATE(
    AVERAGE(
        'DATASET-Singapore Flat Prices'[Purchase price]
```

```
    ),
    FILTER(
        //table or expression returning a table
        //the ALL function prevents it from being affected by
        context filters
        ALL( 'DATASET-Singapore Flat Prices' ),
        //filter
        'DATASET-Singapore Flat Prices'[Year of construction]
        <=  MAX( 'DATASET-Singapore Flat Prices'[Year of con
        struction] )
    )
)
```

011. Harmonic average

We will calculate the "harmonic average" of the purchase
prices collected in the "DATASET-Singapore Flat Prices"
table.

STEP 1
Table tools > new column

```
//denominator
Harmonic mean (numeral ordinal) =
DIVIDE(
        //numerator
        1,
        //denominator
        'DATASET-Singapore Flat Prices'[Purchase price]
)
```

STEP2
Modeling > new measure

```
//numerator
Harmonic mean (Numeral cardinal) =
```

```
COUNT( 'DATASET-Singapore Flat Prices'[Harmonic mean
        (numeral ordinal)]
)
```

STEP 3
Modeling > new measure

```
Harmonic mean =
DIVIDE(
    //numerator
    [Harmonic mean (Numeral cardinal)],
    //denominator
    SUM( 'DATASET-Singapore Flat Prices'[Harmonic mean
        (numeral ordinal)] )
)
```

012. Conditional averaging (+1 condition)
Modeling > new measure

```
Average M2 - Adjoined flat in BEDOK (1) =
CALCULATE(
    //expression
    AVERAGE(
        'DATASET-Singapore Flat Prices'[floor_area_M2]
    ),
    //first filter
    FILTER(
        //table or expression returning a table
        'DATASET-Singapore Flat Prices',
        //filter
        'DATASET-Singapore Flat Prices'[flat_model] =
        "Adjoined flat"
    ),
    //second filter
    FILTER(
```

```
    //table or expression returning a table
    'DATASET-Singapore Flat Prices',
    //filter
    'DATASET-Singapore Flat Prices'[town] = "BEDOK"
  )
)
```

013. Conditional averaging (1 condition)
Modeling > new measure

```
Average M2 - Adjoined flat =
CALCULATE(
    //expression
    AVERAGE(
        'DATASET-Singapore Flat Prices'[floor_area_M2]
    ),
    //filter
    FILTER(
      //table or expression returning a table
      'DATASET-Singapore Flat Prices',
      //filter
      'DATASET-Singapore Flat Prices'[flat_model] =
      "Adjoined flat"
    )
)
```

014. Conditional averaging (filtering a table 1)
Table tools > new table

```
Average M2 per town =
SUMMARIZE(
   //table
   'DATASET-Singapore Flat Prices',
   //grouping criteria
   'DATASET-Singapore Flat Prices'[town],
```

13

```
//expression
   "Avg M2", AVERAGE( 'DATASET-Singapore Flat
Prices'[floor_area_M2] )
)
```

015. Conditional averaging (filtering a table 2)
Table tools > new table

```
Average M2 per town and flat model =
SUMMARIZE(
   //table
   'DATASET-Singapore Flat Prices',
   //first grouping criteria
   'DATASET-Singapore Flat Prices'[town],
   //second grouping criteria
   'DATASET-Singapore Flat Prices'[flat_model],
   //expression
   "Avg M2", AVERAGE( 'DATASET-Singapore Flat
Prices'[floor_area_M2] )
)
```

016. Conditional averaging (filtering a table 3)
Modeling > new measure

```
Average M2 - Adjoined flat in BEDOK (2) =
AVERAGEX(
   //table or expression returning a table
   CALCULATETABLE(
      //table or expression returning a table
      'DATASET-Singapore Flat Prices',
      //filters
      'DATASET-Singapore Flat Prices'[town] = "BEDOK",
      'DATASET-Singapore Flat Prices'[flat_model] =
      "Adjoined flat"
   ),
```

```
//expression
'DATASET-Singapore Flat Prices'[floor_area_M2]
)
```

017. Moving average for the last N periods
Modeling > new measure

```
Moving Average -Last N period =
//number of periods (days)
VAR sampleSize = 200

//last date
VAR maxDate =
MAX( 'DATASET-Singapore Flat Prices'[Last sale date] )

//moving average
VAR mAverage =
AVERAGEX(
   FILTER(
      //table or expression returning a table
      'DATASET-Singapore Flat Prices',
      //filter
      AND(
         'DATASET-Singapore Flat Prices'[Last sale date]
         > maxDate - sampleSize,
         'DATASET-Singapore Flat Prices'[Last sale date]
         <= maxDate
      )
   ),
   //expression
   'DATASET-Singapore Flat Prices'[Purchase price]
)

return

ROUND( mAverage, 0 )
```

018. Moving average by date
Modeling > new measure

```
Moving Average -per Date =
//last date
VAR maxDate =
MAX( 'DATASET-Singapore Flat Prices'[Last sale date] )

//moving average
VAR mAverage =
AVERAGEX(
    //table or expression returning a table
    FILTER(
        //table or expression returning a table
        'DATASET-Singapore Flat Prices',
        //filter
        'DATASET-Singapore Flat Prices'[Last sale date]
        <= maxDate
    ),
    //expression
    'DATASET-Singapore Flat Prices'[Purchase price]
)

return

ROUND(
    //value
    mAverage,
    //number of decimals
    0
)
```

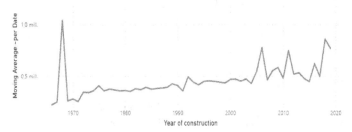

Moving Average -per Date

019. Moving average per record
Modeling > new measure

Moving Average -per Registry =
//last record
VAR maxRegistry =
MAX('DATASET-Singapore Flat Prices'[Registry number])

//moving average
VAR mAverage =
AVERAGEX(
   //table or expression returning a table
   FILTER(
      //table or expression returning a table
      'DATASET-Singapore Flat Prices',
      //filter
      'DATASET-Singapore Flat Prices'[Registry number]
      <= maxRegistry
   ),
   'DATASET-Singapore Flat Prices'[Purchase price]
)

return

ROUND(
      //value
      mAverage,

17

```
//number of decimals
    0
)
```

020. Weighted average

In this case, we will work with the "Singapore Investment" table. This table shows the investments made in the purchase of properties and the annual profitability of each one obtained through their rental.

STEP 1

The first calculation shows the percentage of the investment in each property with respect to the total invested.

Table tools > new column

```
Percentage of total invested =
//total invested
Var totalInvestment =
SUM( 'Singapore Investment'[Purchase price] )

return

ROUND(
    //value
    DIVIDE(
            //numerator
            'Singapore Investment'[Purchase price],
            //denominator
            totalInvestment
    ),
    //number of decimals
    2
)
```

STEP 2
Now, the ROI is calculated in relation to the cost of each investment compared to the total amount invested.

Table tools > new column

Relative ROI =
'Singapore Investment'[Percentage of total invested] *
'Singapore Investment'[annual_ROI]

STEP 3
And finally, the weighted average is obtained through the sum of the column obtained in STEP 2.

Modeling > new measure

Weighted average =
SUM('Singapore Investment'[Relative ROI])

021. Mean
Modeling > new measure

Purchase prices Average =
MEDIAN(
        'DATASET-Singapore Flat Prices'[Purchase price]
)

022. Conditional mean
Modeling > new measure

Average sales in BEDOK =
MEDIANX(
    //table or expression returning a table

```
CALCULATETABLE(
    //table or expression returning a table
    'DATASET-Singapore Flat Prices',
    //filter
    'DATASET-Singapore Flat Prices'[town] = "BEDOK"
),
//expression
'DATASET-Singapore Flat Prices'[Purchase price]
)
```

023. Trend (Numerical value)

Table tools > new table

```
Rooms Number (Mode) =
//number of apartments with the same number of
bedrooms
VAR summaryTable =
SUMMARIZE(
    //table or expression returning a table
    'DATASET-Singapore Flat Prices',
    //group by
    'DATASET-Singapore Flat Prices'[roomNumber],
    //calculated columns
    "flatNumber", COUNT( 'DATASET-Singapore Flat
Prices'[roomNumber])
)

//most repeated value
VAR tableMode =
FILTER(
    //table or expression returning a table
    summaryTable,
    //filter
    [flatNumber] = MAXX( summaryTable, [flatNumber] )
)
```

return

tableMode

024. Trend (Text value)
Table tools > new table

```
Flat Model (Mode) =
//number of floors for each model
VAR summaryTable =
SUMMARIZE(
    //table or expression returning a table
    'DATASET-Singapore Flat Prices',
    //group by
    'DATASET-Singapore Flat Prices'[flat_model],
    //calculated columns
    "flatModel", COUNTA( 'DATASET-Singapore Flat
Prices'[flat_model])
)

//most repeated value
VAR tableMode =
FILTER(
    //table or expression returning a table
    summaryTable,
    //filter
    [flatModel] = MAXX( summaryTable, [flatModel] )
)

return

tableMode
```

025. Conditional trend
Table tools > new table

```
Rooms Number Standard Model (Mode) =
//number of floors with the same number of rooms as
standard model
VAR summaryTable =
SUMMARIZE(
    //table or expression returning a table
    CALCULATETABLE(
        //table or expression returning a table
        'DATASET-Singapore Flat Prices',
        //conditions
        'DATASET-Singapore Flat Prices'[flat_model] =
        "Standard"
    ),
    //group by
    'DATASET-Singapore Flat Prices'[roomNumber],
    //calculated columns
    "flatNumber", COUNT( 'DATASET-Singapore Flat
Prices'[roomNumber])
)

//most repeated value
VAR tableMode =
FILTER(
    //table or expression returning a table
    summaryTable,
    //filter
    [flatNumber] = MAXX( summaryTable, [flatNumber] )
)

return

tableMode
```

026. Frequency
STEP 1

Modeling > new measure

Frequency of purchase of a standard model apartment =
DIVIDE(
  //numerator
  COUNTX(
    //table or expression returning a table
    FILTER(
      //table or expression returning a table
      'DATASET-Singapore Flat Prices',
      //filter
      'DATASET-Singapore Flat Prices'[flat_model] =
      "Standard"
    ),
    //expression
    'DATASET-Singapore Flat Prices'[flat_model]
  ),
  //denominator
  COUNT('DATASET-Singapore Flat Prices'[flat_model])
)

STEP 2
Put the result obtained in STEP 1 in percentage format.

027. Combinatorial
Modeling > new measure

Permutation =
//number of items
VAR elementNumber = 50

//number of elements grouped by combination

VAR permutNumber = 2

return

PERMUT(elementNumber, permutNumber)

028. Range
Modeling > new measure

Price range =
//create variable with maximum value
VAR value_Max =
MAX('DATASET-Singapore Flat Prices'[Purchase price])

//create variable with minimum value
VAR value_Min =
MIN('DATASET-Singapore Flat Prices'[Purchase price])

return

value_Max - value_Min

029. Standard deviation
Modeling > new measure

Standard deviation on purchase prices =
//the larger the quantity returned by the measurement,
the lower the homogeneity of the data set
STDEV.P('Singapore Investment'[Purchase price])

Note:
STDEV.P -when calculated on the population
STDEV.S -when calculated on a sample

030. Moving standard deviation

STEP 1

Modeling > new measure
Moving standard deviation on purchase prices =
//sample size
VAR periodNumber = 200

//total purchases
VAR totalPurchase =
SUM('DATASET-Singapore Flat Prices'[Purchase price])

return

STDEVX.S(
    //table or expression returning a table
    DATESINPERIOD(
        Calendary[Date],
        //fecha inicio
        MAX(Calendary[Date]),
        //number of terms. Positive value, forward. Negative
        value, backward
        -periodNumber,
        //time unit
        DAY
    ),
    totalPurchase
)

STEP 2
On the canvas, the following fields are moved to a table:

- Calendary[Date]
- Singapore Investment[Purchase price] (select ADD
  option)
- [Moving standard deviation on purchase prices]

25

Note:
STDEVX.P -when calculated on the population
STDEVX.S -when calculated on a sample

031. Kurtosis
STEP 1

Modeling > new measure

```
Kurtosis =
VAR __avg =
AVERAGEX(
        //table or expression returning a table
        ALL('DATASET-Singapore Population'),
        //expression
        [Weight (kg)]
)
VAR __stddev =
STDEVX.P(
        //table or expression returning a table
        ALL('DATASET-Singapore Population'),
        //expression
        [Weight (kg)]
)

VAR __n =
COUNTROWS(
        //table or expression returning a table
        ALL('DATASET-Singapore Population')
)

VAR __table =
ADDCOLUMNS(
        //table or expression returning a table
        'DATASET-Singapore Population',
        //calculated columns
```

```
          "__skew", POWER(
                    //base number
                    ([Weight (kg)]-__avg),
                    //exponent number
                    4
                )
)

VAR __sum = SUMX(
                //table or expression returning a table
                __table,
                //expression
                [__skew]
            )

return

DIVIDE(__sum,POWER(__stddev,4),0) * DIVIDE(1,__n,0)
```

STEP 2

Modeling > new measure

Excess Kurtosis = [Kurtosis] - 3

STEP 3

Modeling > new measure

```
Kurtosis Type =
SWITCH(TRUE(),
    //Leptokurtic
    [Excess Kurtosis]>0,"Leptokurtic",
    //Platykurtic
    [Excess Kurtosis]<0,"Platykurtic",
```

```
//Mesokurtic
"Mesokurtic"
)
```

032. Variance over a sample

Calculation made in the "DATASET-World Population" table.

Table tools > new column

```
Student distribution from Med.Age (1) =
T.DIST(
        //sample
        'DATASET-World Population'[Med.Age],
        //deviation degrees
        2,
        //accumulative value
        FALSE()
)
```

033. Variance over population

Modeling > new measure

```
World population variance =
//iterator version of the function (VARX.P)
VAR.P('DATASET-World Population'[Population])
```

034. Covariance

STEP 1

Determine a relationship between the price and the number of rooms of the properties located in the city of Bedok.

The first step will be to obtain a table with all the properties located in Bedok.

Table tools > new table

```
Apartaments located in Bedok =
CALCULATETABLE(
    //table or expression returning a table
    'DATASET-Singapore Flat Prices',
    //filter
    'DATASET-Singapore Flat Prices'[town] = "BEDOK"
)
```

STEP 2
Calculate covariance

Modeling > new measure

```
Covariance =
//sample size
VAR countR =
COUNTROWS( 'Apartaments located in Bedok' )

VAR AvgRoomNumber =
AVERAGEX(
        //table or expression returning a table
        'Apartaments located in Bedok',
        //expression
        'Apartaments located in Bedok'[roomNumber]
)

VAR AvgPurchasePrize =
AVERAGEX(
        //table or expression returning a table
        'Apartaments located in Bedok',
        //expression
```

29

```
        'Apartaments located in Bedok'[Purchase price]
)

VAR temp =
ADDCOLUMNS(
    //table or expression returning a table
    'Apartaments located in Bedok',
    //calculated columns
    "covarianceValue",
    DIVIDE(
        //numerator
        ('Apartaments located in Bedok'[roomNumber] –
        AvgRoomNumber ) *
        ('Apartaments located in Bedok'[Purchase price] –
        AvgPurchasePrize ),
        //denominator
        countR
    )
)

return

SUMX(
    //table
    temp,
    //column
    [covarianceValue]
)
```

035. Percentile

Modeling > new measure

```
Percentage 0.75 on investments =
//75% of investments are less than or equal to the
amount returned by the measure.
PERCENTILE.INC(
```

```
        //table[column]
        'Singapore Investment'[Purchase price],
        //percentage value
        0.75
)
```

036. Bowley's Coefficient of Asymmetry

The column "'DATASET-Singapore Flat Prices'[Purchase price]" will be used to calculate the Bowley asymmetry coefficient.

STEP 1
Average calculation.

Modeling > new measure

```
Average Purchase Price Flat =
AVERAGE( 'DATASET-Singapore Flat Prices'[Purchase price])
```

STEP 2
Calculation of the first and third quarter: Q1 and Q3

Modeling > new measure

```
Q1 =
PERCENTAGEE.INC(
        //table[column]
        'DATASET-Singapore Flat Prices'[Purchase price],
        //percentage value
        0.25
)
```

Modeling > new measure
Q3 =
PERCENTAGEE.INC(
        //table[column]
        'DATASET-Singapore Flat Prices'[Purchase price],
        //percentage value
        0.75
)

STEP 3
Bowley's formula.

Modeling > new measure

Bowley =
DIVIDE(
    //numerator
    ([Q3] + [Q1]) - (2 * [Average Purchase Price Flat]),
    //denominator
    [Q3] - [Q1]
)

STEP 4
Interpretation:
- If Bowley's skewness coefficient is positive, the distribution is positively skewed.
- If Bowley's skewness coefficient is negative, the distribution is negatively skewed.
- If Bowley's skewness coefficient is zero, the distribution is symmetric.

037. Pearson's Coefficient of Asymmetry

STEP 1

Modeling > new measure

```
Pearson =
//average
VAR Avg =
AVERAGE(
    'DATASET-Singapore Flat Prices'[Purchase price]
)

//Mean
VAR Med =
AVERAGE( 'DATASET-Singapore Flat Prices'[Purchase
price])

//sample standard deviation
VAR St_Desv_S =
STDEV.S( 'DATASET-Singapore Flat Prices'[Purchase price])

return

DIVIDE(
    //numerator
    3 * (Avg - Med),
    //denominator
    St_Desv_S
)
```

STEP 2
Interpretation:
- If the skewness coefficient is positive, it means that the distribution is positively skewed.
- If the skewness coefficient is negative, it means that the distribution is negatively skewed.

- If the skewness coefficient is equal to zero, it means that the distribution is symmetrical.

NOTE:
It can only be used in uniform, unimodal and moderately asymmetric distributions.

Symmetric distribution   Skewed distribution with positive bias   Skewed distribution with negative bias

038. Pearson's Correlation Coefficient
STEP 1
Calculate the covariance. -Work on the covariance exercise 033.

STEP 2

Modeling > new measure

Pearson's Correlation Coefficient =
//calculation of the standard deviation (population) on the number of rooms
VAR STDEVRoomNumber =
STDEV.P('Apartaments located in Bedok'[roomNumber])

//calculation of the standard deviation (population) over the purchase price
VAR STDEVPurchasePrize =
STDEV.P('Apartaments located in Bedok'[Purchase price])

```
//measurement created in case 033 of covariance
VAR Cov = [Covariance]

return

ROUND(
    //value
    DIVIDE(
        //numerator
        Cov,
        //denominator
        STDEVRoomNumber * STDEVPurchasePrize
    ),
    //number of decimals
    2
)
```

039. Standard normal distribution

Case worked on the 'DATASET-World Population' table.

This measure has a mean of zero and a standard deviation of one.

Table tools > new column

```
Standard normal distribution from Med.Age =
//TRUE (accumulated distribution function)
//FALSE (mass function of probability)
NORM.S.DIST(
        //table[column]
        'DATASET-World Population'[Med.Age],
        //accumulative
        FALSE()
)
```

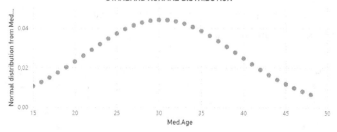

STANDARD NORMAL DISTRIBUTION

040. Normal distribution for the specified average and standard deviation

Calculation made in the "DATASET-World Population" table.

Table tools > new column

```
Normal distribution from Med.Age =
//calculation of the arithmetical average
VAR _avg =
AVERAGE( 'DATASET-World Population'[Med.Age] )

//Calculation of the standard deviation -STDEV.P
(population) -STDEV.S (sample)
VAR desvStd =
STDEV.P( 'DATASET-World Population'[Med.Age] )

return

NORM.DIST(
        //table[column]
        'DATASET-World Population'[Med.Age],
        //average
        _avg,
        //standard deviation
        desvStd,
        //TRUE (accumulated distribution function)
```

```
      //FALSE (mass function of probability)
      FALSE()
)
```

041. Standard normal cumulative distribution (inverse)
Modeling > new measure

```
Cumulative standard normal distribution from Med.Age =
//probability
VAR _probability = 0.7

return

NORM.S.INV( _probability )
```

042. Normal cumulative distribution for specified average and standard deviation.
Modeling > new measure

```
Inverse normal distribution from Med.Age =
//calculation of the arithmetical average
VAR _avg =
AVERAGE( 'DATASET-World Population'[Med.Age] )

//Calculation of the standard deviation -STDEV.P
(population) -STDEV.S (sample)
VAR _desvStd =
STDEV.P( 'DATASET-World Population'[Med.Age] )

//probability
VAR _probability = 0.5

return
```

NORM.INV(_probability, _avg, _desvStd)

043. Poisson distribution

Calculation made in the "DATASET-World Population" table.

Table tools > new column

Poisson distribution from Med.Age =
POISSON.DIST(
        //number of event occurrences
        'DATASET-World Population'[Med.Age],
        //number of times expected to occur during a
        given interval   2,
        //TRUE (accumulated distribution function)
        //FALSE (mass function of probability)
        FALSE()
)

044. Exponential distribution

Calculation made in the "DATASET-World Population" table.

Table tools > new column

Exponential distribution corresponding to a Med.Age =
EXPON.DIST(
    //value on which the exponential distribution is calcu
    lated
    'DATASET-World Population'[Med.Age],
    //distribution lambda parameter
    2,
    //TRUE (accumulated distribution function)
    //FALSE (mass function of probability)

        FALSE
)

045. Student's bilateral t-distribution
Calculation made in the "DATASET-World Population"
table.

Table tools > new column

Student distribution from Med.Age (2) =
T.DIST.2T(
        //sample
        'DATASET-World Population'[Med.Age],
        //deviation degrees
        2
)

046. Left-tailed Student's t-distribution
Calculation made in the "DATASET-World Population"
table.

Table tools > new column

Student distribution from Med.Age (1) =
T.DIST(
        //sample
        'DATASET-World Population'[Med.Age],
        //deviation degrees
        2,
        //TRUE (accumulated distribution function)
        //FALSE (mass function of probability)
        FALSE()
)

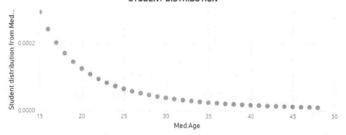

STUDENT DISTRIBUTION

047. Right-tailed Student's t-distribution

Calculation made in the "DATASET-World Population" table.

Table tools > new column

Student distribution from Med.Age (3) =
T.DIST.RT(
        //sample
        'DATASET-World Population'[Med.Age],
        //deviation degrees
        2
)

048. Chi-square distribution

Calculation made in the "DATASET-World Population" table.

Table tools > new column

Chi-square distribution from Med.Age (1) =
CHISQ.DIST(
        //sample
        'DATASET-World Population'[Med.Age],
        //deviation degrees
        2,

```
//TRUE (accumulated distribution function)
//FALSE (mass function of probability)
FALSE()
)
```

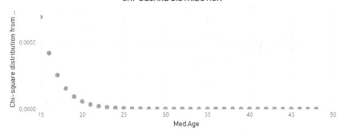

049. Inverse of the right-tailed probability of the chi-square distribution.

STEP 1

This calculation can only be applied to values between 0 and 1.

For this example we will work on a table that represents the "Med.Age" over the total number of countries.

Table tools > new table

```
PopulationPerAge =
VAR totalCountry =
DISTINCTCOUNT(
    'DATASET-World Population'[Country (or dependency)]
)

return

SUMMARIZE(
    //table or expression returning a table
```

```
'DATASET-World Population',
//group by column
'DATASET-World Population'[Med.Age],
//calculated columns
"Representation",
 DIVIDE(
    //numerator
    COUNT('DATASET-World Population'[Med.Age]),
    //denominator
    totalCountry
 )
)
```

STEP 2
Table tools > new column

```
Chi-square distribution from Med.Age (4) =
CHISQ.INV.RT(
   PopulationPerAge[Representation],
   1
)
```

050. Inverse of the left-tailed probability of the chi-square distribution.
This calculation can only be applied to values between 0 and 1.
For this example we will work on a table that represents the "Med.Age" over the total number of countries.

STEP 1
Table tools > new table

```
PopulationPerAge =
//number of countries
```

```
VAR totalCountry =
DISTINCTCOUNT(
    'DATASET-World Population'[Country (or dependency)]
)

return

SUMMARIZE(
   //table or expression returning a table
   'DATASET-World Population',
   //group by column
   'DATASET-World Population'[Med.Age],
   //calculated columns
   "Representation",
   DIVIDE(
       COUNT( 'DATASET-World Population'[Med.Age]),
       totalCountry
   )
)
```

STEP 2

Now, in the table created in STEP 1, we create a new column.

Table tools > new column

```
Chi-square distribution from Med.Age (3) =
CHISQ.INV(
   PopulationPerAge[Representation],
   1
)
```

051. Right-tailed probability of chi-squared distribution.
Calculation made in the "DATASET-World Population" table.

Table tools > new column

Chi-square distribution from Med.Age (2) =
CHISQ.DIST.RT(
        //sample
        'DATASET-World Population'[Med.Age],
        //deviation degrees
        2
)

052. ABC Classification
STEP 1
Grouping and totaling data.

Table tools > new table

ABC Purchase prices =
SUMMARIZE(
   //table o expresion que devuelve una tabla
   'Singapore Investment',
   //group by column
   'Singapore Investment'[Town],
   //totalize column
   "purchasePrice",
   SUM('Singapore Investment'[Purchase price])
)

STEP 2
Sorting and classifying data.

Table tools > new column

```
Ranking =
//ranking of purchases from highest to lowest
RANKX(
    //table
    'ABC Purchase prices',
    //column
    [purchasePrice], ,
    //order
    DESC
)
```

STEP 3
Calculate the accumulated total of purchases.

Table tools > new column

```
Accumulated purchase =
//result rounded to two decimal places and sorted by rank
CALCULATE(
    //expression
    ROUND( SUM( [purchasePrice] ), 2 ),
    //filter
    FILTER(
        //table or expression returning a table
        //not affected by context filters
        ALL('ABC Purchase prices'),
        //filter
        'ABC Purchase prices'[Ranking] <=
        EARLIER( 'ABC Purchase prices'[Ranking] )
    )
)
```

STEP 4
Calculate cumulative percentage of purchases.

Table tools > new column

```
Accumulated purchase (%) =
//result rounded to two decimals
ROUND(
    //value
    DIVIDE(
    //numerator
    'ABC Purchase prices'[Accumulated purchase],
    //denominator
    SUM( [purchasePrice] )
    ),
    //number of decimals
    2
)
```

STEP 5
Assigning values to the classification.

Table tools > new column

```
ABC =
//assignment of categories based on STEP 3
SWITCH(
    TRUE(),
    //conditions to be fulfilled
    [Accumulated purchase (%)] <= 0.7, "A",
    [Accumulated purchase (%)] <= 0.9, "B",
    //conditions not fulfilled
    "C"
)
```

053. Bayes Theorem

STEP 1

From the "DATASET Singapore Market by Town" we will calculate the probability that the sale of a property will occur per town by the expected margin.

To do this, we start by calculating the total probability of the condition being met by each town.

Table tools > new column

```
Probability per Town =
ROUND(
 //expression
 'DATASET Singapore Market by Town'[Sales Probability] *
 'DATASET Singapore Market by Town'[Profit Probability],
 //number of decimals
 2
)
```

STEP 2

The total probability is then calculated.

Modeling > new measure

```
Total probability =
CALCULATE(
   //expression
   SUM( 'DATASET Singapore Market by Town'[Probability per Town] ),
   //filter
   ALL('DATASET Singapore Market by Town')
)
```

STEP 3

We obtain the result of Bayes Theorem.

Table tools > new column

```
Bayes' theorem =
DIVIDE(
   //numerator
   'DATASET Singapore Market by Town'[Probability per Town],
   //denominator
   [Total probability]
)
```

054. Gauss Theorem

This case will work from the "Weight (kg)" column of the "Singapore Poblation" dataset and the intervals obtained in the Sturges case 056.

STEP 1

Create an interval table for the (x) axis of the Gaussian plot.

Table tools > new table

```
Axis (y) intervals table =
//maximum value
VAR weightMax = MAX( 'DATASET-Singapore
Population'[Weight (kg)] )

//minimum value
VAR weightMin = MIN( 'DATASET-Singapore
Population'[Weight (kg)] )

//increment - Sturges rule (case 056)
VAR increase = [Interval between categories]

return

GENERATESERIES(
```

```
//minimum value
weightMin,
//maximum value
weightMax,
//increase
increase
)
```

STEP 2
Calculation of average weight (kg).

Modeling > new measure

```
Average weight (kg) =
AVERAGE( 'DATASET-Singapore Population'[Weight (kg)] )
```

STEP 3
Calculation of standard deviation of weight (kg)

Modeling > new measure

```
Standard deviation (kg) =
STDEV.S( 'DATASET-Singapore Population'[Weight (kg)] )
```

STEP 4
Calculation of the normal distribution as a new column of the "Axis (x) intervals table".

Table tools > new column

```
normalDistribution =
//average weight (kg)
VAR avgWeight = [Average weight (kg)]

//standard deviation
```

VAR desvStandard = [Standard deviation (kg)]

return

```
NORM.DIST(
    //eje "y"
    'Axis (y) intervals table'[Value],
    //average
    avgWeight,
    //standard deviation
    desvStandard,
    //accumulative value
    FALSE()
)
```

STEP 5
Transfer the columns of the table to a scatter graph "Axis (x) intervals table".
-Eje (x) = Value
-Eje (y) = normalDistribution

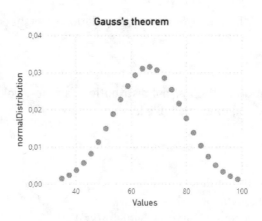

055. Tchebyshev Theorem

Calculation of the "Tchebyshev Theorem" on the age of the population collected in the "DATASET-World Population" table.

To calculate the theorem, it is required to obtain the "average" and the "standard deviation" beforehand.

STEP 1

Calculation of the "Avg".

Modeling > new measure

Avg_value =
AVERAGE('DATASET-World Population'[Med.Age])

STEP 2

Calculation of the "standard deviation".

Modeling > new measure

StdDesv_value =
STDEV.S('DATASET-World Population'[Med.Age])

STEP 3

Calculation of the theorem. It indicates the percentage of comments that fall within the interval from (Avg - k Standard Deviations) to (Avg + k Standard Deviations).

Modeling > new measure

T_Tchebyshev =
//number of standard deviations we are going to take
VAR k_value = 2

VAR num_ordinal = POWER(k_value,2)

VAR Fraction = DIVIDE(1, num_ordinal)

return

(1 - Fraction)

STEP 4
Calculation of the positive interval.

Modeling > new measure

T_Tchebyshev -positive interval =
//number of standard deviations we collected in STEP 3
VAR k_value = 2

return

//(Avg + k Standard deviations)
[Avg_value] + k_value * [StdDesv_value]

STEP 5
Calculation of the negative interval.

Modeling > new measure

T_Tchebyshev -negative interval =
//number of standard deviations we collected in STEP 3
VAR k_value = 2

return

//(Avg - k Standard deviations)
[Avg_value] - k_value * [StdDesv_value]

Teorema de Tchebyshev

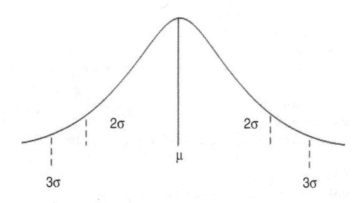

056. Sturges rule (K) -Interval calculation

The Sturges rule (K) calculates the number of categories by which a dataset can be grouped.

In this case we are going to work from the "Weight (kg)" column of the "Singapore Poblation" dataset.

STEP 1
Modeling > new measure

Sturges =
//sample size
VAR samplingSize =
COUNTROWS('DATASET-Singapore Population')

return

//K = 1 + 3,322 * Log N
1 + 3.322 * LN(samplingSize)

STEP 2
Calculation of the interval between each category.

Interval between categories =
//maximum value
VAR weightMax =
MAX('DATASET-Singapore Population'[Weight (kg)])

//minimum value
VAR weightMin =
MIN('DATASET-Singapore Population'[Weight (kg)])

//Range
VAR range = weightMax - weightMin

```
return
ROUND(
    DIVIDE(
        //numerator
        range,
        //denominator
        [Sturges]
    ),
    //number of decimals
    2
)
```

057. Laspeyres Index

Calculation of the Laspeyres index on the price variation of three-room apartments in the city of Bedok in 2010 compared to 1985.

STEP 1
Create a table that filters by requirements.

Table tools > new table

```
Bedok flats 3 room =
SELECTCOLUMNS(
    CALCULATETABLE(
        //table or expression returning a table
        'DATASET-Singapore Flat Prices',
        //conditions
        'DATASET-Singapore Flat Prices'[town] = "BEDOK",
        'DATASET-Singapore Flat Prices'[roomNumber] = 3,
        'DATASET-Singapore Flat Prices'[Year of construction]
        IN {1985, 2010}
        ),
        //selected column 1
        "Date",
        'DATASET-Singapore Flat Prices'[Year of construction],
        //selected column 2
        "Purchase",
        'DATASET-Singapore Flat Prices'[Purchase price]
)
```

STEP 2
Create a measure to calculate the index.

Modeling > new measure
```
Laspeyres' Index =
//Period
VAR reference_year = 1985
VAR comparison_year = 2010

//total purchases
VAR purchase_0 =
CALCULATE(
        //expression
        SUM('Bedok flats 3 room'[Purchase]),
        //filter
```

```
        'Bedok flats 3 room'[Date]=reference_year
)

VAR purchase_1 =
CALCULATE(
        //expression
        SUM('Bedok flats 3 room'[Purchase]),
        //filter
        'Bedok flats 3 room'[Date]=comparison_year
)

//number of floors
VAR flatsN_0 =
CALCULATE(
        //expression
        COUNT('Bedok flats 3 room'[Purchase]),
        //filter
        'Bedok flats 3 room'[Date]=reference_year
)

return

DIVIDE(
        //numerator
        purchase_1 * flatsN_0,
        //denominator
        purchase_0 * flatsN_0
)
* 100
```

058. Paasche Index

Calculate the Paasche index on the price variation of three-room apartments in the city of Bedok in 2010 compared to 1985.

STEP 1
Create a table that filters by requirements.

Table tools > new table

```
Bedok flats 3 room =
SELECTCOLUMNS(
    CALCULATETABLE(
        //table or expression returning a table
        'DATASET-Singapore Flat Prices',
        //conditions
        'DATASET-Singapore Flat Prices'[town] = "BEDOK",
        'DATASET-Singapore Flat Prices'[roomNumber] = 3,
        'DATASET-Singapore Flat Prices'[Year of construction]
        IN {1985, 2010}
        ),
        //selected column 1
        "Date",
        'DATASET-Singapore Flat Prices'[Year of construction],
        //selected column 2
        "Purchase",
        'DATASET-Singapore Flat Prices'[Purchase price]
)
```

STEP 2
Create a measure to calculate the index.

Modeling > new measure

```
Paasche Index =
//Period
VAR reference_year = 1985
VAR comparison_year = 2010

//total purchases
VAR purchase_0 =
CALCULATE(
```

```
        //expression
        SUM('Bedok flats 3 room'[Purchase]),
        //filter
        'Bedok flats 3 room'[Date]=reference_year
)

VAR purchase_1 =
CALCULATE(
        //expression
        SUM('Bedok flats 3 room'[Purchase]),
        //filter
        'Bedok flats 3 room'[Date]=comparison_year
)

//number of floors
VAR flatsN_0 =
CALCULATE(
        //expression
        COUNT('Bedok flats 3 room'[Purchase]),
        //filter
        'Bedok flats 3 room'[Date]=reference_year
)

VAR flatsN_1 =
CALCULATE(
        //expression
        COUNT('Bedok flats 3 room'[Purchase]),
        //filter
        'Bedok flats 3 room'[Date]=comparison_year
)

return

DIVIDE(
        //numerator
        purchase_1 * flatsN_1,
        //denominator
```

```
    purchase_0 * flatsN_1
)
* 100
```

059. Gini Index

The Gini index takes values between 0 and 1; it takes a value of 0 when the variable is very homogeneously distributed and a value of 1 when it is highly concentrated.

For its calculation we are going to work with the table "Singapore_Salary_Range".

STEP 1

Create a calculated column in the table "Singapore_Salary_Range".

Table tools > new column

```
Cumulative_population =
VAR range =  [Salary range (from)]

return

CALCULATE(
   //expression
   SUM(Singapore_Salary_Range[Population]),
   //filter
   FILTER(
     //table or expression returning a table
     ALL(Singapore_Salary_Range),
     Singapore_Salary_Range[Salary range (from)]<= range
   )
)
```

STEP 2
Create a calculated column in the table "Singapore_Salary_Range".

Table tools > new column

Cumulative population (%) =
VAR range = [Salary range (from)]

VAR totalPopulation = SUM([Population])

return

```
DIVIDE(
  CALCULATE(
    SUM( [Population] ),
    FILTER(
      ALL( Singapore_Salary_Range ),
      Singapore_Salary_Range[Salary range (from)] <=
      range
    )
  ),
  totalPopulation
)
```

STEP 3
Create a calculated column in the table "Singapore_Salary_Range".

Table tools > new column

Average salary range =
```
DIVIDE(
  [Salary range (from)] + [Salary range (up to)],
  2
)
```

STEP 4
Create a calculated column in the table "Singapore_Salary_Range".

Table tools > new column

Population x Average salary range =
[Population]*[Average salary range]

STEP 5
Create a calculated column in the table "Singapore_Salary_Range".

Table tools > new column

Population x Average salary range (cumulative %) =
VAR range = [Salary range (from)]

VAR Population_x_Average_salary_range = SUM(
[Population x Average salary range])

return

DIVIDE(
  //numerator
  CALCULATE(
    //expression
    SUM([Population x Average salary range]),
    //filter
    FILTER(
      //table or expression returning a table
      //-ALL- avoids the application of context filters
      ALL(Singapore_Salary_Range),
      //filter
      Singapore_Salary_Range[Salary range (from)] <=
      range

```
      )
   ),
   //denominator
   Population_x_Average_salary_range
)
```

STEP 6
Create a calculated column in the table "Singapore_Salary_Range".

Table tools > new column

```
Cumulative population (%) - Population x Average salary
range (cumulative %) =
[Cumulative population (%)] –
[Population x Average salary range (cumulative %)]
```

STEP 7
Modeling > new measure

```
Gini =
DIVIDE(
//numerator
SUM( Singapore_Salary_Range[Cumulative population (%)
- Population x Average salary range (cumulative %)] ),
//denominator
SUM( Singapore_Salary_Range[Cumulative population
(%)] ) -1
)
```

060. Trend line
STEP 1

Modeling > new measure

```
totalPurchase =
SUM( 'DATASET-Singapore Flat Prices'[Purchase price] )
```

STEP 2
Modeling > new measure

```
Regression =
//define fields
VAR Val =
FILTER (
  SELECTCOLUMNS (
    ALLSELECTED('Calendary'[Date]),
    "Val[X]", 'Calendary'[Date],
    "Val[Y]", [totalPurchase]
  ),
  AND (
    NOT ( ISBLANK ( Val[X] ) ),
    NOT ( ISBLANK ( Val[Y] ) )
  )
)

VAR CountR = COUNTROWS ( Val )

VAR Sum_X = SUMX ( Val, Val[X] )

VAR Sum_X2 = SUMX ( Val, Val[X] ^ 2 )

VAR Sum_Y = SUMX ( Val, Val[Y] )

VAR Sum_XY = SUMX ( Val, Val[X] * Val[Y] )

VAR Avg_X = AVERAGEX ( Val, Val[X] )

VAR Avg_Y = AVERAGEX ( Val, Val[Y] )
```

```
VAR Earring =
DIVIDE (
  //numerator
  CountR * Sum_XY - Sum_X * Sum_Y,
  //denominator
  CountR * Sum_X2 - Sum_X ^ 2
)

VAR Intersection = Avg_Y - Earring * Avg_X

return

(Intersection + Earring) * SELECTEDVALUE (
'Calendary'[Date] )
```

STEP 3
Represent the result on a line graph.

Eje_x: 'Calendary'[Date]
Eje_y: [Regression]
Eje_y: [totalPurchase]

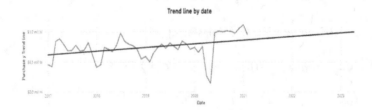

061. Generate an arithmetic progression of N values
with increment X
Table tools > new table

```
Arithmetic progression =
//returns a table with a single column containing the
values of an arithmetic progression
GENERATESERIES(
        //initial_value
        1,
        //final_value
        100,
        //incremental
        2
)
```

062. Values below a measurement
Modeling > new measure

```
Purchases below average =
VAR totalPurchases =
SUMX(
        //table or expression returning a table
        ALLSELECTED( 'DATASET-Singapore Flat Prices'),
        //expression
        'DATASET-Singapore Flat Prices'[Purchase price]
)
VAR AvgPurchases =
AVERAGEX(
    //table or expression returning a table
    ALLSELECTED( 'DATASET-Singapore Flat Prices'[town] ),
    //expression
    totalPurchases
)

return

IF(
    //condition
    AvgPurchases > totalPurchases,
```

```
//result if the condition is fulfilled
DIVIDE(
        //numerator
        totalPurchases,
        //denominator
        AvgPurchases
    )-1,
    //result in case condition is NOT met
    BLANK()
)
```

063. Values above a measurement

Modeling > new measure

```
Purchases below average =
VAR totalPurchases =
SUMX(
        //table or expression returning a table
        ALLSELECTED( 'DATASET-Singapore Flat Prices'),
        //expression
        'DATASET-Singapore Flat Prices'[Purchase price]
)
VAR AvgPurchases =
AVERAGEX(
    //table or expression returning a table
    ALLSELECTED( 'DATASET-Singapore Flat Prices'[town] ),
    //expression
    totalPurchases
)

return

IF(
  //condition
  AvgPurchases > totalPurchases,
  //result if the condition is fulfilled
```

```
DIVIDE(
    //numerator
    totalPurchases,
    //denominator
    AvgPurchases
  ) -1,
    //result in case condition is NOT met
    BLANK()
)
```

064. Maximum value per category

Table tools > new table

```
Most recent sale by town =
SUMMARIZE(
    //table or expression returning a table
    'DATASET-Singapore Flat Prices',
    //group by
    'DATASET-Singapore Flat Prices'[town],
    //expression
    "salesDate",
    MAX( 'DATASET-Singapore Flat Prices'[Last sale date] )
)
```

065. Minimum value per category

Table tools > new table

```
Oldest sale by town =
SUMMARIZE(
    //table or expression returning a table
    'DATASET-Singapore Flat Prices',
    //group by
    'DATASET-Singapore Flat Prices'[town],
    //expression
    "salesDate",
```

MIN('DATASET-Singapore Flat Prices'[Last sale date])
)

066. Number of cells of a column which are not empty
Modeling > new measure

Number of NO blanks =
//counting the number of values excluding blank fields
CALCULATE(
     //expression
     COUNT(DATASET_MOSAIC[Values]),
     //filter
     DATASET_MOSAIC[Values]<>BLANK()
)

067. Number of blank cells in a column
Modeling > new measure

Number of blanks =
//count empty fields in a column
//affecting context filters
COUNTBLANK(DATASET_MOSAIC[Values])

068. Number of rows in the specified table or in a table defined by an expression
Modeling > new measure

Number of rows in a table =
COUNTROWS(DATASET_MOSAIC)

069. Number of unique values in a column
Modeling > new measure

```
Unique values =
DISTINCTCOUNT( DATASET_MOSAIC[Values] )
```

070. Top N concepts (1)
Table tools > new table

```
Top 2 cities with the highest investment (1) =
//we create a variable that returns a table
VAR purchase =
SUMMARIZE (
        //table
        'DATASET-Singapore Flat Prices',
        //group by criteria
        'DATASET-Singapore Flat Prices'[town],
        //expression
        "totalPurchase",
        SUM ( 'DATASET-Singapore Flat Prices'[Purchase price] )
)
return

TOPN (
        //number of cities
        2,
        //table
        purchase,
        //expression
        [totalPurchase]
)
```

071. Top N concepts (2)
Modeling > new measure

Total invested in the 2 cities with the highest investment
(2) =

```
//use table obtained in case 068
SUM('Top 2 most expensive cities (1)'[totalPurchase])
```

072. Top N concepts (3)
Table tools > new table

```
Top 2  high purchases in PUNGGOL town (3) =
//create a variable containing a table with only the
purchases in PUNGGOL
VAR flatPurchase =
CALCULATETABLE(
      //table or expression returning a table
      SUMMARIZE (
          //table
          'DATASET-Singapore Flat Prices',
          //group result by criteria 1
          'DATASET-Singapore Flat Prices'[town],
          //group result by criteria 2
          'DATASET-Singapore Flat Prices'[street_name],
          //expression
          "totalPurchase",
          SUM (
            'DATASET-Singapore Flat Prices'[Purchase price]
          )
      ),
      'DATASET-Singapore Flat Prices'[town] = "PUNGGOL"
)

return

TOPN (
      //number of investments
      2,
      //table
      flatPurchase,
      //expression
```

```
    [totalPurchase]
)
```

073. Ranking N concepts (1)
Modeling > new measure

```
Purchase ranking (1) =
//returns the position (range) of each resulting value
RANKX(
    //table[column]
    //The ALL function prevents the application of context
    filters.
    ALL('DATASET-Singapore Flat Prices'[Town]),
    //expression to determine the ranking
    SUM( 'DATASET-Singapore Flat Prices'[Purchase price]),,
    //order
    DESC
)
```

074. Ranking N concepts (2)
Modeling > new measure

```
Salesman ranking (2) =
//displays the ranking of investments for the selected year
//not affected by other context filters
CALCULATE(
  //expression
  RANKX(
   //table[column]
   //-ALL- avoids the application of context filters
   ALL('DATASET-Singapore Flat Prices'[Town),
   //expression to determine the ranking
   SUM( 'DATASET-Singapore Flat Prices'[Purchase price]),,
   //order
   DESC
```

```
),
//filter
ALLSELECTED('Calendary'[year])
)
```

075. Ranking N concepts (3)
Modeling > new measure

```
Purchase ranking (3) =
IF(
  //allows working with hierarchies
  //table[column]
  ISINSCOPE('DATASET-Singapore Flat Prices'[Town]),
  RANKX(
   //table[column]
   //-ALL- avoids the application of context filters
   ALL('DATASET-Singapore Flat Prices'[Town]),
   //expression to determine the ranking
   SUM('DATASET-Singapore Flat Prices'[Purchase price]),,
  ),
  IF(
    //allows working with hierarchies
    //table[column]
    ISINSCOPE(
    'DATASET-Singapore Flat Prices'[street_name]
    ),
    RANKX(
      //table[column]
      //-ALL- avoids the application of context filters
      ALL('DATASET-Singapore Flat Prices'),
      SUM('DATASET-Singapore Flat Prices'[Purchase
      price] )
    )
  )
)
```

076. Inverse ranking N concepts

Modeling > new measure

```
Bottom Ranked Flats Purchases per Town =
//ranking of the 3 investments with the least amount of
capital
//create a variable containing the following measurement
VAR totalPurchase =
SUM('DATASET-Singapore Flat Prices'[Purchase price])

//create a table that filters unique values
VAR purchaseTable =
FILTER(
    //table or expression returning a table
    VALUES('DATASET-Singapore Flat Prices'[Town]),
    //filter
    totalPurchase > 0
)

return

CONCATENATEX(
    //value 1
    TOPN(
        //number of investments
        3,
        //table
        purchaseTable,
        //expression
        totalPurchase,
        //order
        ASC
    ),
        //value 2
        'DATASET-Singapore Flat Prices'[Town],
        //delimiter
        ", "
```

)

077. Square root of one number
Modeling > new measure

Square root of a number =
//square root of one value
VAR _sr = 25

return

SQRT(_sr)

078. Power of a number
Modeling > new measure

Raising a number to a power (1) =
POWER(
    //value
    5,
    //exponent
    2
)

079. Number raised to an exponent
Modeling > new measure

Raising a number to a power (2) =
//"base" value
5
//symbol - "raised to".
^

//"exponent" value
2

080. Rounding a figure down to its nearest significant
multiple

STEP 1
Create a test table

Table tools > new table

DecimalNumber =
//creates a table with an interval from 1 to 10 with an
increment of 0.25
GENERATESERIES(
        //minimum value of the range
        1,
        //max value of the range
        10,
        //incremental value
        0.25
)

STEP 2
Table tools > new column

ROUND DOWN (1) =
//round a number to the nearest significant multiple
downward
FLOOR(
        //table[column]
        DecimalNumber[Value],
        //multiple_value
        0.10
)

081. Rounding a figure up to its nearest significant multiple

To develop the case, we start from the table created in case 078 (STEP 1).

Table tools > new column

ROUND UP (1) =
//round a number to the nearest significant multiple upwards
//table[column],multiply_value
CEILING(
        //table[column]
        DecimalNumber[Value],
        //multiple_value
        0.10
)

082. Round a digit to the nearest whole number equal to or less than the nearest whole number.

To develop the case, we start from the table created in case 078 (STEP 1).

Table tools > new column

ROUND UP/DOWN (1) =
//round a number to the nearest whole number equal to or less than the whole number.
//table[column]
INT(DecimalNumber[Value])

083. Round a digit to the nearest whole number equal to or less than the nearest whole number.
To develop the case, we start from the table created in case 078 (STEP 1).

Table tools > new column

ROUND (1) =
//returns the whole part of a number
//table[column]
TRUNC(DecimalNumber[Value])

084. Round a figure down specifying number of decimal places
To develop the case, we start from the table created in case 078 (STEP 1).

Table tools > new column

ROUND DOWN (2) =
//round a number to zero
ROUNDDOWN(
        //table[column]
        DecimalNumber[Value],
        //decimal_number
        2
)

085. Round a figure up by specifying number of decimal places
To develop the case, we start from the table created in case 078 (STEP 1).

Table tools > new column

```
ROUND UP (2) =
//rounding a number farther away from zero
ROUNDUP(
        //table[column]
        DecimalNumber[Value],
        //decimal_number
        2
)
```

086. Rounding a figure to a number of decimal places

To develop the case, we start from the table created in case 078 (STEP 1).

Table tools > new column

```
ROUND =
//round a figure to the specified number of decimal places
ROUND(
        //table[column]
        DecimalNumber[Value],
        //decimal_number
        2
)
```

087. Round to the nearest multiple (lower or higher)

To develop the case, we start from the table created in case 078 (STEP 1).

Table tools > new column

ROUND TO DECIMALS=

```
//round a figure to the specified number of decimal places
MROUND(
        //table[column]
        DecimalNumber[Value],
        //decimal_number
        2
)
```

Chart types

LINE CHARTS
Line charts are used in the detection of trends or changes occurring along a time line.

PIE CHART
Pie charts are used to show parts of a whole. A pie chart represents a segmentation of the circumference into percentages, with the sum total of all segments being 100% of the circumference.

BAR CHARTS
Bar or column charts are used to compare different elements. These can be represented either horizontally or vertically. Bar charts are generally used if you have more than 10 items to compare or also to show the variation of a value along a time line.

BOX PLOT
Rectangle or box plots show parts of a set. They show hierarchical information as a group of rectangles that change in size and color, depending on their data value. The size of each rectangle represents a quantity, while the color may represent a numerical value or a category.

AREA CHART
Area charts behave just like line charts, except that the space between the line and the axis are filled with volume. The area chart as well as the line chart shows changes along a time line, as well as the trend.

PYRAMID CHART
Pyramid charts are presented in horizontal sections with categories labeled according to their hierarchy. Orientation can be presented in two directions: upward or downward based on the data being represented.

WORD CLOUD

Tag clouds are a type of ranked list. They display text in different font sizes, weights or colors as a method of showing frequencies or categories.They facilitate the identification of trends and patterns.

TABLES

Tables display data in rows and columns. They facilitate the comparison of pairs from related values or the display of quantitative information.

MATRICES

They are very similar to tables but unlike these, which work in two dimensions, matrices allow you to work in three or more dimensions and establish a hierarchy in the data.

Glossary

AVERAGE (009,010,012,013,014,015,037,040,042,054,..)
AVERAGEX (016,017,018,019,031,034,060,062,063)
CEILING (081)
CHISQ.DIST (048)
CHISQ.DIST.RT (051)
CHISQ.INV (050)
CHISQ.INV.RT (049)
CONFIDENCE.NORM (007)
CONFIDENCE.T (008)
COUNT (011,023,025,026,049,050,057,058,066)
COUNTX (026)
COUNTBLANK (067)
COUNTROWS (003,006,007,008,031,034,056,060,068)
DISTINCTCOUNT (049,050,069)
DIVIDE (003,006,007,008,011,020,026,031,034,036,037,..)
EXPON.DIST (044)
FILTER (005,010,012,013,017,018,019,023,024,025,026,..)
FLOOR (080)
GENERATE (005)
INT (082)
MAX (010,017,018,019,028,030,054,056,064)
MAXX (023,024,025)
AVERAGE (021,036,037)
AVERAGEX (022)
MIN (028,054,056,065)
MROUND (087)
NORM.DIST (040,054)
NORM.INV (042)
NORM.S.DIST (039)
NORM.S.INV (041)
PERCENTAGEE.INC (035,036)
PERMUT (027)
POISSON.DIST (43)
POWER (003,031,055,078)
RANKX (052,073,074,075)

ROUND (017,018,019,020,038,052,053,056,086,087)
ROUNDDOWN (084)
ROUNDUP (085)
SAMPLE (004,005)
SQRT (077)
STDEV.P (029,038,040,042)
STDEV.S (006,007,008,037,054,055)
STDEVX.P (030,031)
STDEVX.S (030)
SUM (011,020,030,052,053,057,058,..)
SUMMARIZE (014,015,023,024,025,049,050,052,064,065)
SUMX (031,034,062,063)
T.DIST (032)
T.DIST.2T (045)
T.DIST.RT (047)
TRUNC (083)
VAR.P (033)

www.ingramcontent.com/pod-product-compliance
Lightning Source LLC
LaVergne TN
LVHW051535050326
832903LV00033B/4265